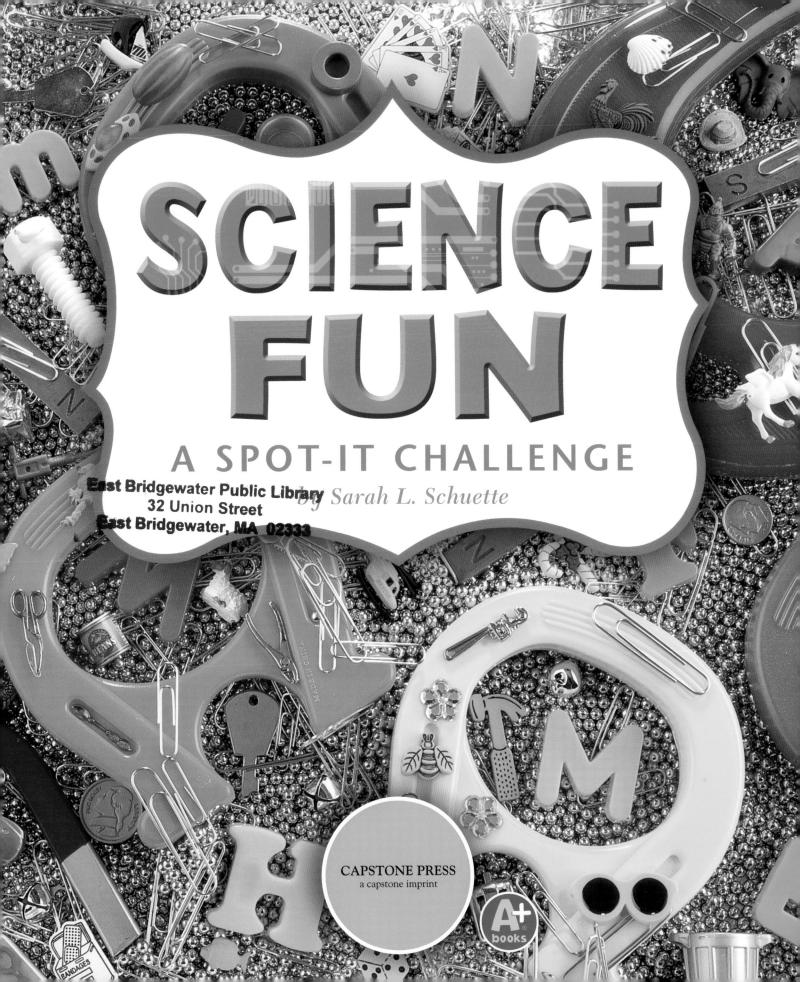

# SCIENCE FUN

## A SPOT-IT CHALLENGE

by *Sarah L. Schuette*

CAPSTONE PRESS
a capstone imprint

A+ books

A+ Books are published by Capstone Press,
1710 Roe Crest Drive, North Mankato, Minnesota 56003.
www.capstonepub.com

Books published by Capstone Press are manufactured with paper
containing at least 10 percent post-consumer waste.

*Library of Congress Cataloging-in-Publication Data*
Schuette, Sarah L., 1976–
  Science-fun : a spot-it challenge / by Sarah L. Schuette.
    p. cm. — (A+ books. Spot it)
  Includes bibliographical references.
  Summary: "Simple text invites the reader to find items hidden in science-themed
photographs"— Provided by publisher.
  ISBN 978-1-4296-5986-4 (library binding)
  1.  Science—Juvenile literature. 2.  Technology—Juvenile literature.  I. Title. II. Series.
  Q163.S456 2012
  793.73—dc23                                              2011016408

**Editorial Credits**

Jeni Wttrock, editor; Ted Williams, designer; Eric Manske, production specialist;
    Sarah Schuette, photo stylist; Marcy Morin, photo scheduler

**Photo Credits**

all photos by Capstone Studio/Karon Dubke

The author dedicates this book in memory of her aunt, Ruthy Hilgers.

**Note**
**to Parents, Teachers, and Librarians**

Spot It is an interactive series that supports literacy development and reading enjoyment. Readers
utilize visual discrimination skills to find objects among fun-to-peruse, science-themed photographs
with busy backgrounds. Readers also build vocabulary through thematic groupings, develop visual
memory ability through repeated readings, and improve strategic and associative thinking skills by
experimenting with different visual search methods.

Printed in the United States of America in North Mankato, Minnesota.
042012        006691R

# Table of Contents

# Fossil Dig

Can you spot ...

- a spatula?
- an acorn?
- a clothes pin?
- a golf tee?
- two marshmallows?
- a walrus?

# Space

Can you spot ...
- a toucan?
- a jellyfish?
- a spider?
- a panda?
- two stingrays?
- a witch hat?

7

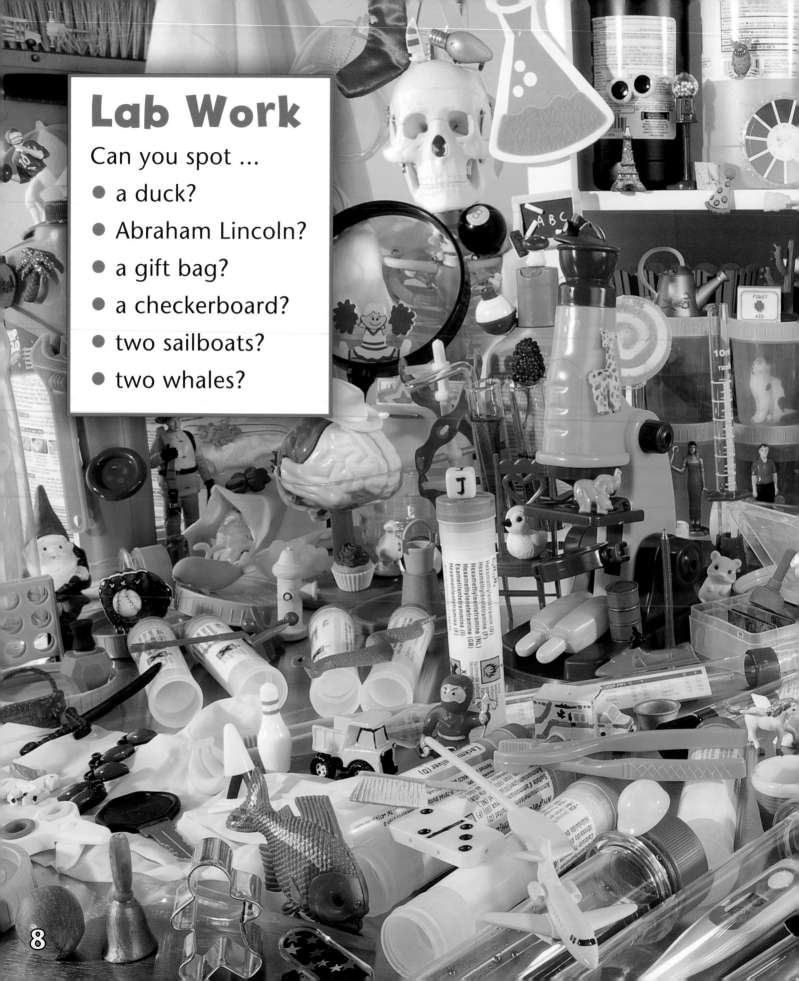

# Lab Work

Can you spot ...

- a duck?
- Abraham Lincoln?
- a gift bag?
- a checkerboard?
- two sailboats?
- two whales?

# Here's the Gear

Can you spot ...
- a basketball?
- a fancy dress?
- a candle?
- a lighthouse?
- a surfboard?
- a crown?

# Bots

Can you spot ...
- a beach ball?
- a butterfly?
- a snorkel?
- two webs?
- a moose?
- a blimp?

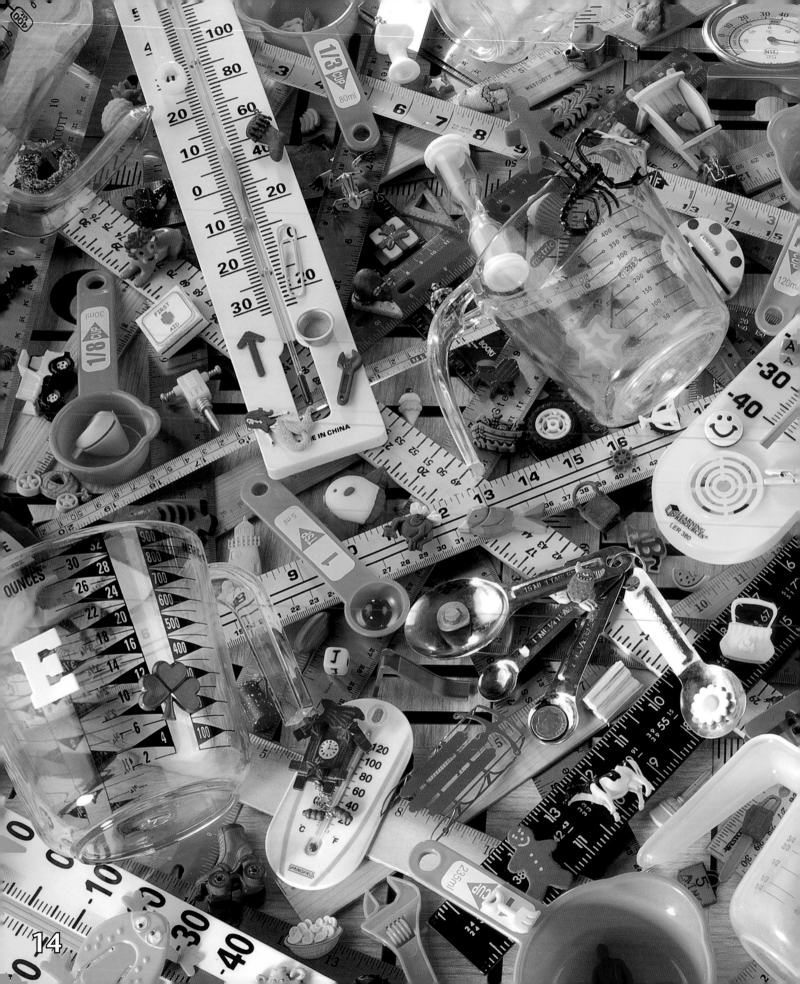

14

# Measure It

Can you spot ...
- a pineapple?
- a broom?
- a rabbit?
- a pinecone?
- a giraffe?
- a dime?

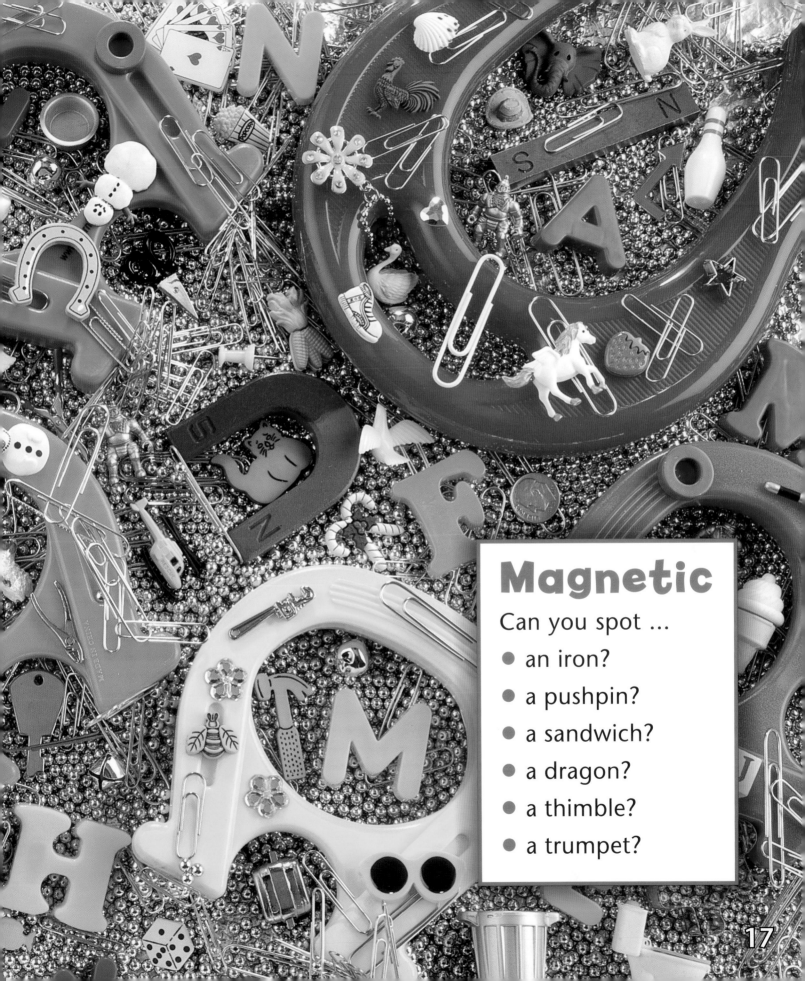

# Magnetic

Can you spot ...

- an iron?
- a pushpin?
- a sandwich?
- a dragon?
- a thimble?
- a trumpet?

# CSI

Can you spot ...

- a grill?
- a mousetrap?
- a laptop?
- a cork?
- a lamb?
- an orca whale?

# Rocks

Can you spot ...

- a flip-flop?
- a dove?
- a motorcycle?
- a seal?
- a golf ball?
- three teddy bears?

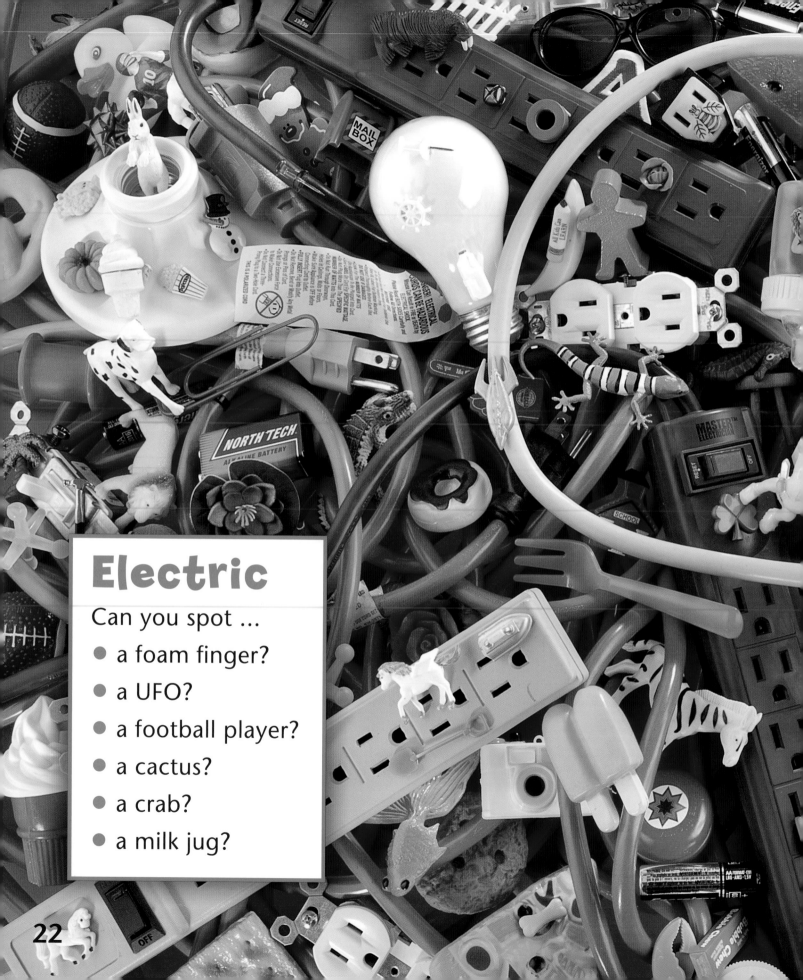

# Electric

Can you spot ...

- a foam finger?
- a UFO?
- a football player?
- a cactus?
- a crab?
- a milk jug?

# Hot/Cold

Can you spot ...

- a matchstick?
- a megaphone?
- a bar of soap?
- a cabbage?
- a frying pan?
- a ghost?

# Plants

Can you spot ...

- a moon?
- Bigfoot?
- a watermelon?
- a plunger?
- a tomato?
- an alien?

27

# Spot Even More!

### Fossil Dig

Try to find three canteens, a penny, a flashlight, two baseball bats, and a cave woman and child.

### Space

Try to find a calculator, a twig, a croissant, the Eiffel Tower, a jack, a ninja, and a record.

### Lab Work

Take another look to find a trash can lid, two traffic cones, a mushroom, a shamrock, and a raspberry.

### Here's the Gear

See if you can find a bunch of grapes, two number 3s, an anchor, a fly, a Christmas bow, and an apple.

### Bots

This time find a fancy cat, a carton of french fries, a whisk, three fire hydrants, a shirt, a pig, and a roller skate.

### Measure It

See if you can spot a bowl of dog food, a playground slide, a baseball glove, and a taco.

## Magnetic

16

Now look for a spoon, a jackhammer, a scissors, a cookie cutter, and a pair of candy canes.

## CSI

18

Now find a peanut, a lion, a hot dog, a bowl of potato chips, a football helmet, and a duckling.

## Rocks

20

Check for two dump trucks, two crutches, a set of keys, a bathtub, two wrenches, two fish, and a snowman.

## Electric

22

Try to spot a fried egg, a Christmas stocking, the Statue of Liberty, and a head of lettuce.

## Hot/Cold

24

Now spot a slice of bread, a red crayon, a flamingo, a shovel, a mop, a mitten, and a cowboy hat.

## Plants

26

Time to find a Christmas wreath, a green turtle, a reindeer, a pickle, a hammer, and a bean.

# Extreme Spot-It Challenge

Just can't get enough Spot-It action?
Here's an extra challenge. Try to spot:

- two shoes
- a watering can
- two pianos
- a pirate hat
- a frozen treat
- a seashell
- a leaf
- a paper clip
- a whistle
- a witch hat
- a ladybug
- a roll of toilet paper
- a bird egg
- three knights
- a toaster
- three elephants
- a soccer ball

# Read More

**Marks, Jennifer L.** *Fun and Games: A Spot-It Challenge.* Spot It. Mankato, Minn.: Capstone, 2009.

**Schuette, Sarah L.** *Animals Everywhere: A Spot-It Challenge.* Spot It. Mankato, Minn.: Capstone, 2011.

# Internet Sites

FactHound offers a safe, fun way to find Internet sites related to this book. All of the sites on FactHound have been researched by our staff.

Here's all you do:

Visit *www.facthound.com*

Type in this code: **9781429659864**

Check out projects, games and lots more at
**www.capstonekids.com**